05/05

short-cuts to
storage

short-cuts to
storage

annemarie meintjes

styled by karen roos

photographed by massimo cecconi

contents

This is not a reading book. It is a

picture book for people who need fresh

inspiration to get their own ideas

rolling, or quick solutions they can copy

at a glance.

It's about saving time, space and

money. Recycling rather than replacing.

Erecting rather than installing.

You'll find storage systems that can

grow with you and move with you, and

a useful address book, which will take

you shopping along the less obvious

routes for affordable basics to turn into

simple storage ideas for every room in

the home or office.

It is simply a matter of styling.

BLOW UP

Hang it.

Box it.

Bag it.

Or get rid of it.

closet
storage

You'll have more energy to do the things you really

want to do once you've cleared the clutter from your

personal space. Wake up to a perfectly organized

wardrobe every morning and the day belongs to

you. And because no two wardrobes, living spaces

or people are exactly alike, the storage solutions

that work are often the simple ideas that anyone

can interpret and make their own.

Canvas organizers

are a quick fix for

closet chaos.

For deep storage

seal off a section

of your wardrobe

with a calico screen.

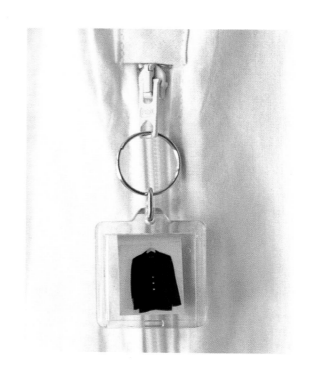

Labelling is sensible

... but it doesn't have to be.

ID tags and clever labels make

storage a visual pleasure.

Loft living creates special storage needs. No clutter

allowed. So how do you live a full life in an empty space?

Good-looking mobile wardrobes provide the solution.

wheeled out of sight

Easy on the eye when you need your clothes, easily

wheeled out of sight when you need your space.

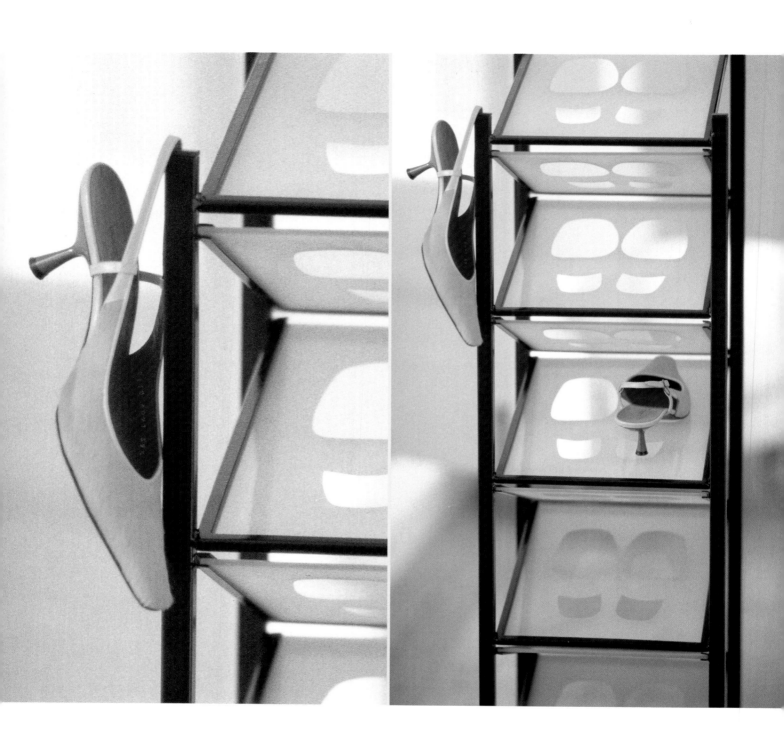

The shoe fits.

Use sheer pockets to bag

fine treasures.

Hide-and

Box the clutter in the kids

and wheel it away under th

Fix wheels to every possible earthbound

design in your home and you'll be able to

shape and reshape your personal space,

on your own, as often as you like. For

add-on storage space on wheels, make a

skate and pile boxes, bins, baskets,

crates or cabinets on top.

Put plastic storage boxes on plastic castors or wheels,

pile them high and wheel into gaps or out of sight.

Remove the backing and mount an ordinary bookcase on

wheels. It provides great storage for magazines, and doubles

as a room divider if you work from home.

Serve meals

on wheels.

After dinner,

lift the lid

to store

the cushions,

then

wheel away.

Computers have made generations of

government-issue furniture obsolete. Typically

designed for sorting and filing, these cabinets

offer endless and interesting storage

possibilities and add character to the right

interior. Wheels add versatility. Use this system

to divide a large space or let it hug the wall.

Keep

it up

and away.

hooks,
pegs and rails

Run a Shaker rail all the way around

any room, just above window height.

Hang anything from it that doesn't

belong on the floor – and some things

that do: curtains, pictures, hats,

coats, towels, pots and pans, and

even chairs.

Buy it ...

or make your own.

Beat badly designed supermarket packaging that blunts the senses. You'll need see-through containers for decanting and suction hooks for display.

One glance tells you where everything is.

Kids want to be organized, too.

A net suspended from the ceiling

tidies the playroom in an instant.

Release it and let the fun begin. This

is the shortest short-cut to lifting

everything off the floor – but resist

the temptation to scoop up the kids

kids want to be organized, too

along with the toys.

Get hooked on grids.

In small or busy kitchens, industrial butcher's hooks and wall-mounted plate racks

leave work surfaces clear and uncluttered.

Stack them high.

Spread them wide.

Sideways or up.

building
blocks

Stacked sideways,

wine racks become

an umbrella stand.

Concrete window blocks were conceived as a total window system, but these concrete surrounds also make useful and robust shelves. Placed upright or sideways, piled high or spread wide, this is a versatile and portable storage solution that you can adapt, extend, dismantle and reassemble – in the next room or your next house.

Here's a concrete alternative, which isn't cast in stone.

Collapsible **crates** take the storage box solution to its

logical conclusion: it's **out of sight when out of use.**

Because storage needs aren't constant, these **clever**

boxes fold flat and take up little space. With the see-

through version **you don't need labels.** But keep these

neat and tidy because everything is on display.

Small wooden boxes from art and hobby shops restore order to a drawer and make an appealing display.

Think twice

before you

throw it away.

packaging

Take two.

Recycle clear

take-away containers

as clever store-alls.

Brushed up,

empty paint tins become

storage bins.

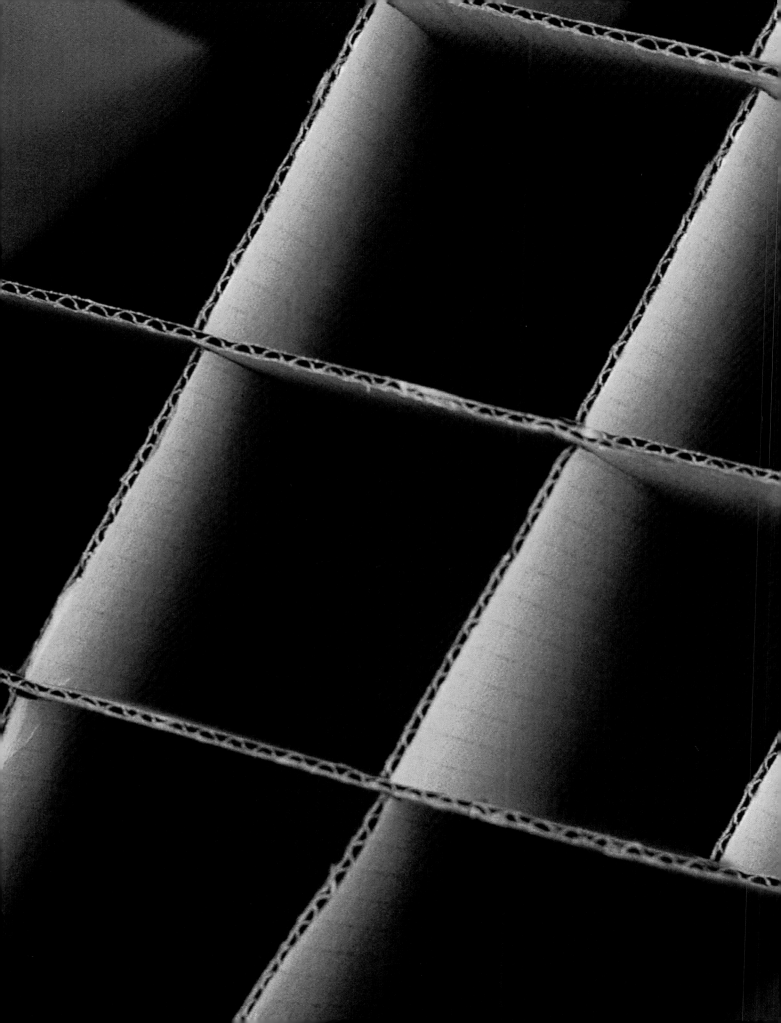

Divide and conquer.

Organize your socks with a cardboard grid

from a wine or mineral water box.

Enjoy form and function with bags of style.

Every now and then we come across

something that just makes life a little

everything falls into place

easier. Something that's as ordinary

as it is unexpected. And suddenly

everything falls into place.

Expect the unexpected.

speciality *shops*

Fit the unfitted kitchen with items borrowed from the butcher, the baker, the doctor and the dentist.

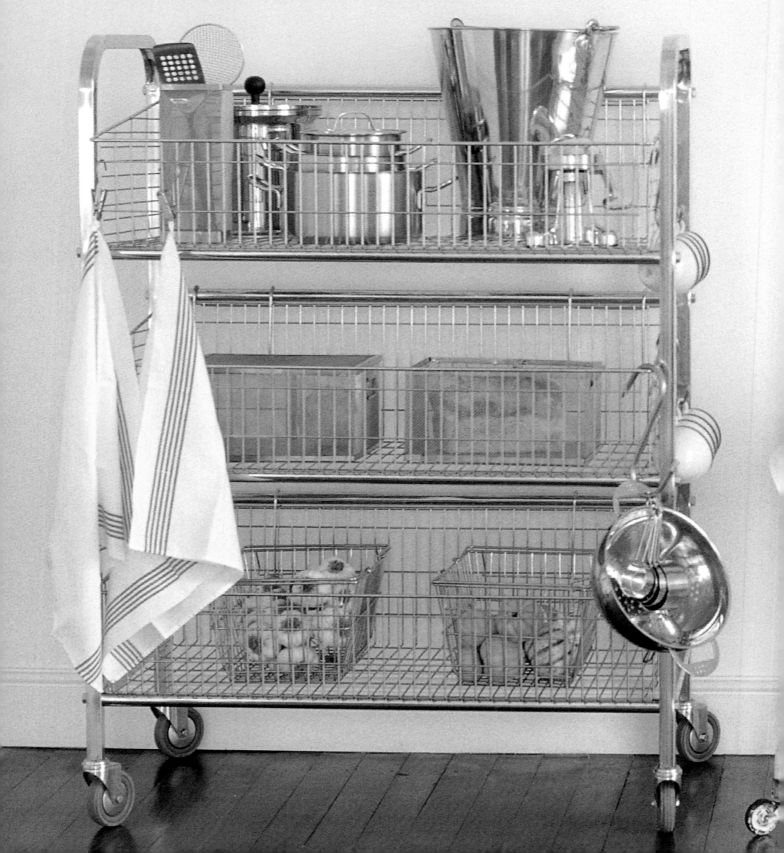

The stainless-steel baker's trolley

Don't store your clothes on hangers that ruin the

fabric and spoil the shape. Visit the experts who

supply the retail clothing industry and invest in

hang it

good-quality hangers that last forever.

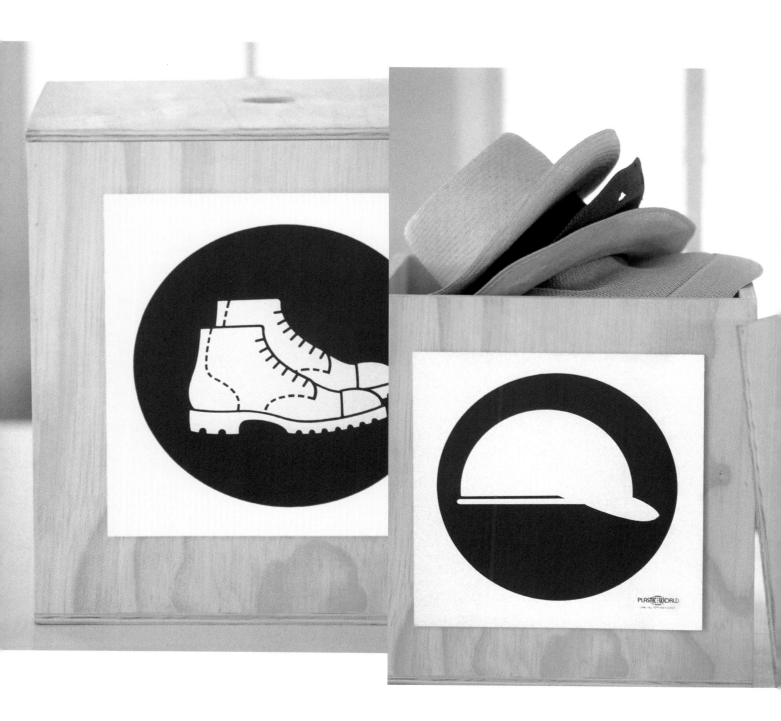

Industrial safety signs make seasonal storage fun.

Test the positive power of flexible magnetic strips

and sheeting to raise storage to new heights.

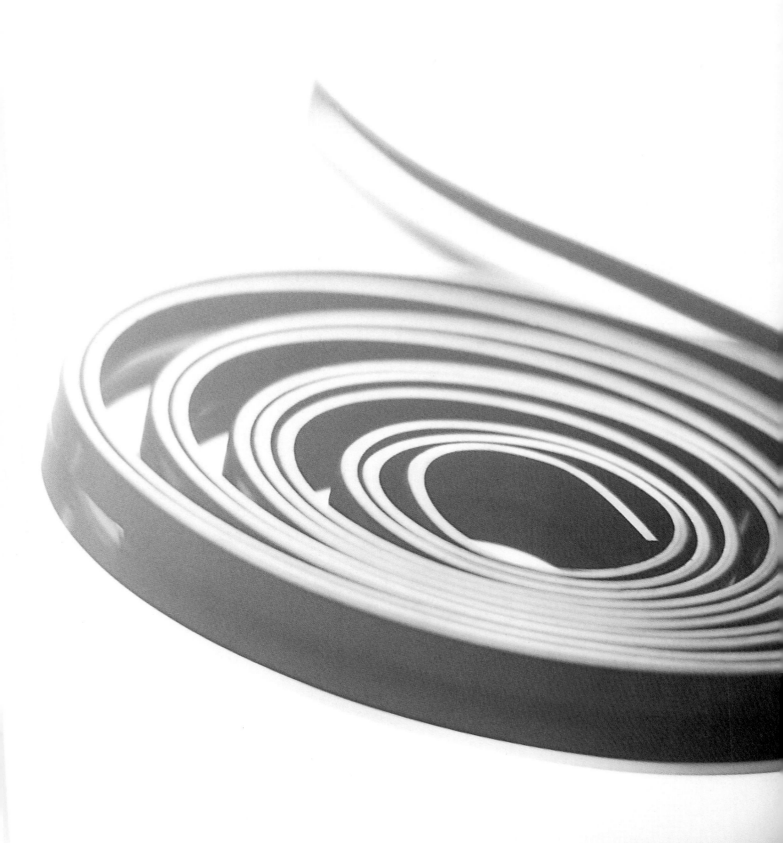

Lots of kids, zero clutter. In this dormitory-

style bedroom, clipboards display a growing

collection of certificates, and treasures are

hoarded in bins.

Mystery.

Transparency.

Intrigue.

reveal
and conceal

'Now you see it, now you don't. Transparency is one of the most intriguing strategies in an interior, because it creates a kind of unifying screen. The object is still present, but at once decisively removed.'

Li Edelkoort (Interior View 14, Blind Design)

Storage on demand: mesh boxes that look good

empty or filled, or mesh pockets that fold flat and

away when not in use.

Life is

unpredictable.

Emergency

storage:

a foldout screen.

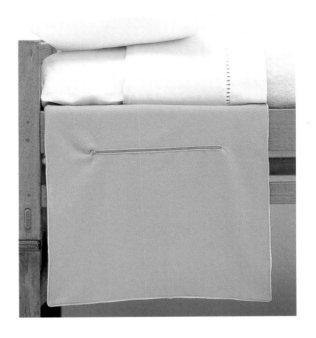

Bed-pockets shelter bedtime comforts.

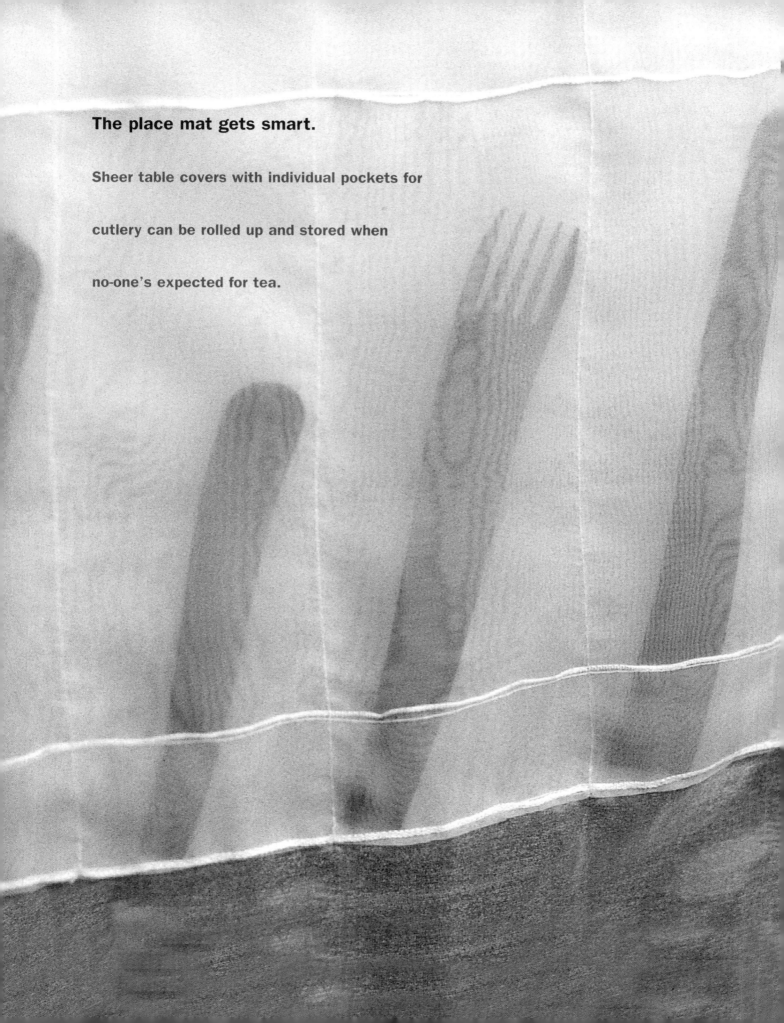

The place mat gets smart.

Sheer table covers with individual pockets for

cutlery can be rolled up and stored when

no-one's expected for tea.

Focus

on your obsessions.

storage *on display*

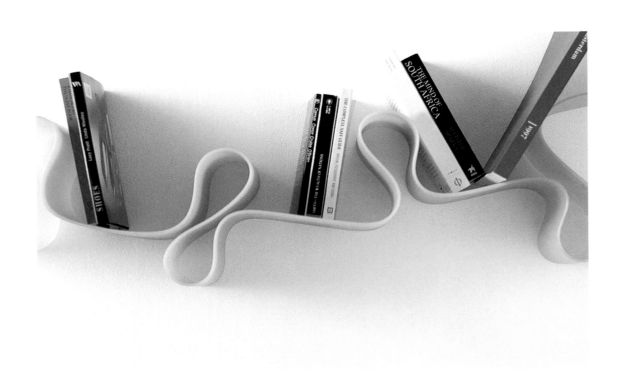

Purely functional units such as first-aid boxes and bookshelves

can become **playful works of art.**

Your memories made you who you are. Don't hide them – they're precious.

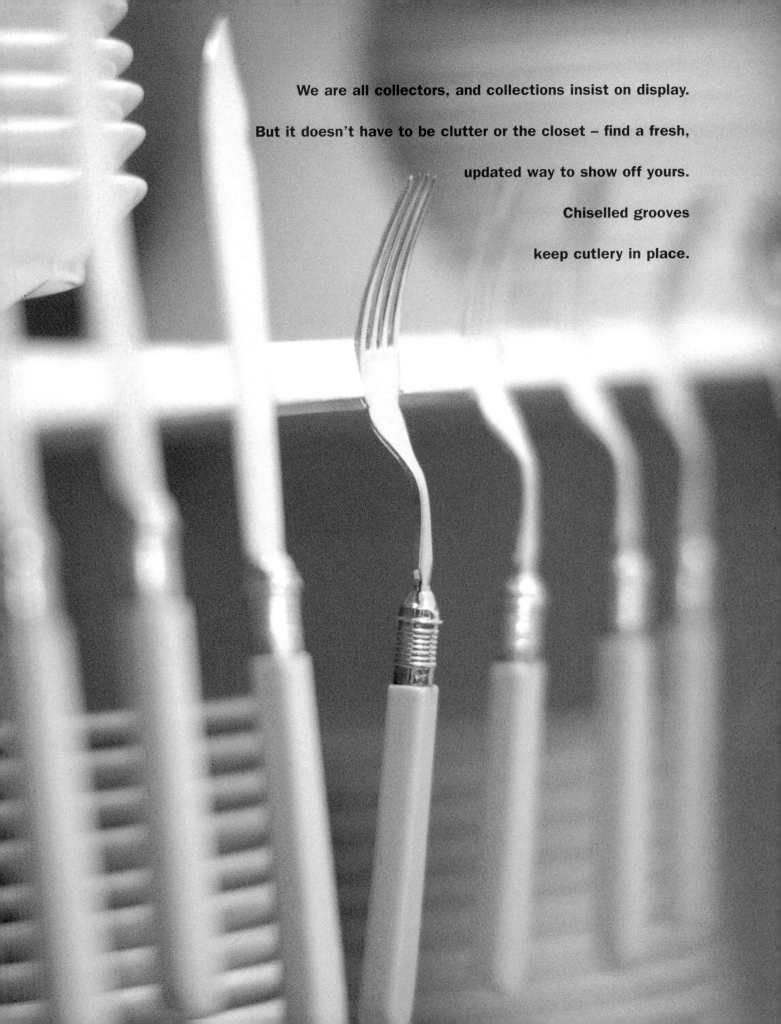

We are all **collectors**, and collections insist on display.

But it doesn't have to be clutter or the closet – find a fresh,

updated way to show off yours.

Chiselled grooves

keep cutlery in place.

Ascending order.

Stacking is a great way

to display. Pile it as

high as you can go.

Revive dull corners or surfaces with stacks of imagination.

database

2

Do not underestimate the power of simple shelving. Great for storage, great for display. Shelving available from all major hardware or timber stores.

4

Roof sheeting offcuts are great for storing wine bottles. Run 30 cm strips side by side along the top of your kitchen cupboards for an instant wine cellar that is safely out of the way. Offcuts available from all large hardware stores.

7

Fit a glass sheet on a bare wall and hang chinese take-away boxes from suction hooks to create an unusual, but functional, display. Glass sheets can be obtained from glaziers, and suction hooks from hardware stores such as **B & Q** (0800 444840), **Focus Do It All** (0800 436436) and **Homebase** (0845 980 1800). Ask your local Chinese take-away if they can give you some unused boxes.

Closet storage

8

Blow-up hangers are not just fun to look at, but also great to avoid hanger points on knitwear and silk shirts. This one is from **Cornucopia Imports**, South Africa (0027 11 482 5759).

11

A wardrobe designed to suit your lifestyle is the ultimate storage solution. Look for local furniture designers in the Yellow Pages. **Ikea** (020 8208 5607) have a range of modular wardrobes. Alternatively, invest in a few storage boxes and garment bags to recreate the look.

12

Canvas organisers are durable, attractive and space-saving. **Habitat** (020 7255 2545), **The Holding Company** (020 7610 9160) and **Ikea** (020 8208 5607) supply organisers for shoes, shirts and sweaters.

13

To seal off a section of your wardrobe for deep storage, use an ordinary blind that can easily be pulled or rolled up, or buy some calico and Velcro from a haberdashery and make a screen. You can pull it open when you need access and stick it back on afterwards.

14

Should you get carried away and end up with your entire wardrobe in calico bags, devise an identification system to retrieve the desired garment. A simple key ring with a Polaroid image of your favourite suit hooked onto the zipper will do the trick.

15

You can have storage boxes tailor-made to suit your needs. Look under packaging in the Yellow Pages and remember that the cost per unit depends on the size of your order. The fewer you order, the more you'll pay. **The Nomad Box Company** (01858 464878) will custom make one-off designs. The following outlets also stock a wide range of boxes in varying sizes: **The Cotswold Company** (0870 550 2233), **Habitat** (020 7255 2545), **The Holding Company** (020 7610 9160),

Ikea (020 8208 5607),
Inventory (020 7937 2626),
Muji (020 7323 2208),
Ocean (0870 242 6283) and
Paperchase (020 7467 6200).
Design your own labels and have
them sandwiched in plastic at
your local photocopy shop. **Kall
Kwik** (01895 872000) have
shops nationwide.

17
Mobile wardrobes and hangers
are available from **Habitat**
(020 7255 2545), **The Holding
Company** (020 7610 9160) and
Ikea (020 8208 5607).

18
Shoe racks designed to fit in
a closet or under short hanging
clothes are available from
The Holding Company
(020 7610 9160).

19
Drawstring shoe bags are easy
to sew and add a special touch
to your wardrobe. If you want
anything printed on the bags,
look for a small T-shirt printing
company in the Yellow Pages or
take the calico to a photocopy
shop before you start sewing.
Kall Kwik (01895 872000) have
photocopy shops nationwide. You
can also buy drawstring bags
from **Ikea** (020 8208 5607) and
The Pier (020 7814 5020).

20
Sheer storage bags are
protective and easy to sew. Buy
organza from any haberdashery
and tie the bag up with ribbons.

21
Crown (01254 704951),
Dulux (01753 550555) and
Leyland Paint (01924 354000)
offer paint for every surface in
the colour and shade of your
choice. Call the above numbers
to find your nearest stockist.

Mobile storage

22
Hardware stores stock a wide
range of wheels and castors.
B & Q (0800 444840), **Focus
Do It All** (0800 436436) or
Homebase (0845 980 1800)
have stores nationwide. **Ikea**
(020 8208 5607) also
sells castors.

24, 25
The space underneath a bed
can be a great storage solution.
Shop around for attractive boxes,
crates or baskets of the right
height. **The Cotswold Company**
(0870 550 2233), **Habitat**
(020 7255 2545), **The Holding
Company** (020 7610 9160),
Ikea (020 8208 5607),
Inventory (020 7937 2626),

Muji (020 7323 2208), **Ocean**
(0870 242 6283) and **Paperchase**
(020 7467 6200) all have a
good selection. Don't forget to
allow for the height added by the
wheels. Wheels are essential for
easy access and quick tidying up
and can be found in stores such
as **B & Q** (0800 444840), **Focus
Do It All** (0800 436436) or
Homebase (0845 980 1800).

26, 27
To have wood cut to size is more
expensive than settling for an
offcut, which is often exactly the
right size. Make a feature of the
wheels: go for outsize rather
than right size. **B & Q** (0800
444840), **Focus Do It All** (0800
436436) and **Homebase** (0845
980 1800) usually have a good
selection of wheels and castors.
Castors can also be bought from
Ikea (020 8208 5607).

28, 29
Neatly stacked boxes are a
practical storage solution, and
work best in multiples. Go for one
style of box, then multiply. Boxes
are available from **The Cotswold
Company** (0870 550 2233),
Habitat (020 7255 2545), **The
Holding Company** (020 7610
9160), **Ikea** (020 8208 5607),
Inventory (020 7937 2626),
Muji (020 7323 2208),
Ocean (0870 242 6283) and

Paperchase (020 7467 6200). Buy castors from **B & Q** (0800 444840), **Focus Do It All** (0800 436436), **Homebase** (0845 980 1800) or **Ikea** (020 8208 5607).

30
Shelving units on wheels are available from **Aero** (020 8971 0066), **The Holding Company** (020 7610 9160) and **Ikea** (020 8208 5607).

31
Make lunch a moveable feast. Mount a large storage basket or box with a lid on wheels and store cushions inside. **The Cotswold Company** (0870 550 2233) and **Next Home** (0845 600 7000) have a good selection of large baskets. Buy wheels or castors from **B & Q** (0800 444840), **Focus Do It All** (0800 436436), **Homebase** (0845 980 1800).

32
Shop around for used furniture with government, post office and railway credentials. Look under furniture–secondhand in the Yellow Pages or scour the Classified section of your local newspaper. A coat of paint and a set of wheels will give them a completely new life. **Crown** (01254 704951),

Dulux (01753 550555) and **Leyland Paint** (01924 354000) offer paint for every surface in the colour and shade of your choice. Look for castors with brakes at hardware stores such as **B & Q** (0800 444840), **Focus Do It All** (0800 436436) and **Homebase** (0845 980 1800).

Hooks, pegs and rails

34
Suction hooks are available from hardware stores such as **B & Q** (0800 444840), **Focus Do It All** (0800 436436) and **Homebase** (0845 980 1800). They stick best to smooth surfaces like glass and tiles, so test them before you trust them.

37
This Shaker-inspired storage system lifts everything off the floor and is especially useful in a kitchen or bathroom. Readymade rails can be bought from **Shaker Ltd** (020 7935 9461) or make your own with a few metres of skirting board and wooden pegs, cut from a dowel stick. Paint and fix to the wall just above window height, all around the room.

38, 39
Diamond style coat racks need not be strictly reserved for coats. Invest in a readymade unit from **The Cotswold Company** (0870 550 2233) or make your own form ordinary garden trellis. Paint it white and add hooks of your choice. Trellis is available at any garden centre and a range of hooks can be found in hardware stores such as **B & Q** (0800 444840), **Focus Do It All** (0800 436436) and **Homebase** (0845 980 1800).

40
Turn plastic strip curtains (used in cold rooms) into bottle hangers. A canvas supplier will heat-seal the divisions between the bottles and add the eyelets to hang it from suction hooks. Plastic strip curtains from **Plastic World**, South Africa (0027 11 493 8492). Find suction hooks at hardware stores such as **B & Q** (0800 444840), **Focus Do It All** (0800 436436) and **Homebase** (0845 980 1800). Wash out old vinegar bottles and decant shampoos and lotions into them.

41

Make clear plastic storage bags and hang them where they can be seen. No more scratching through drawers. Clear plastic is available from graphics and art shops such as **The London Graphic Centre** (020 7240 0095).

43

You'll find net manufacturers in the Yellow Pages. We've used a standard fishing net, snipped off the sinkers and laced a rope through the edges, like one would when making a drawstring bag. A great way of storing balls and soft toys!

44

Hardware stores sell metal mesh sheeting that is perfect for the garage wall or the tool cupboard. You'll never hunt for a pair of scissors again! Or mount a stainless steel grid (even an oven rack will do) on the wall. Try **B & Q** (0800 444840), **Focus Do It All** (0800 436436) and **Homebase** (0845 980 1800) for mesh. Metal grids with accessories are available from **Aero** (020 8971 0066) and **Habitat** (020 7255 2545). Industrial meat hooks are available from butchers and catering supplies. Look in the Yellow Pages under catering equipment suppliers. Shelves and hook accessories are also available from **Ikea** (020 8208 5607).

45

If you have a baker's trolley in your kitchen, buy a few meat hooks from your local butcher and use them to hang whatever you do not have space for in the cupboards. Large hooks are also available from **Ikea** (020 8208 5607). The plate rack was custom made to fit above the kitchen sink. Similar units are available from **Aero** (020 8971 0066), and **Habitat** (020 7255 2545).

Building blocks

46

Concrete window surrounds are manufactured from high-density, low-permeability pre-cast concrete and available in square, rectangular, corner, triangular, quadrant or circular shapes. Contact **Winblok**, South Africa (0027 11 609 8774).

48, 49

Stackable wine racks can be stacked upright, one on top of the other, to make a trendy umbrella stand. Stackable wine racks from **Aero** (020 8971 0066). See Mobile Storage for details of storage boxes on wheels.

50, 51

Rectangular concrete window surrounds can be stacked horizontally or vertically, and combined in imaginative ways to complement architecture and lifestyle. They make great room dividers! For trade enquiries contact **Winblok**, South Africa (0027 11 609 8774).

52, 53

Combine the concrete with the translucent for a clearly contemporary look. Plastic boxes and crates are available from **Habitat** (020 7255 2545), **The Holding Company** (020 7610 9160), **Ikea** (020 8208 5607), **Muji** (020 7323 2208), **Ocean** (0870 242 6283) and **Paperchase** (020 7467 6200).

55

For collapsible storage crates, look in the Yellow Pages for office and catering equipment suppliers.

56, 57, 58, 59
Buy wooden boxes in the raw
and dress them with a coat of
paint in the colour of your
choice. Wooden boxes and
cubes are available from **Habitat**
(020 7255 2545), **The Holding
Company** (020 7610 9160) and
Ikea (020 8208 5607). Contact
Crown (01254 704951), **Dulux**
(01753 550555) or **Leyland
Paint** (01924 354000) to find
your nearest stockist.

Packaging

60
Decant supermarket shampoos
into clear vinegar dispensers.
Collect your own and wash them
out before use.

62, 63
Empty and clean out metal paint
tins to make attractive storage
bins. Spray the tins in the
colour of your choice, then
stencil or take them to a sign-
writer for labelling.

64, 65
Collect the clear plastic
containers that takeaway food
is served in. Clean them out
and use them to store all sorts
of objects.

66, 67
Boxes are in generous supply at
your local supermarket. The grids
from bottled drink boxes fit
perfectly into a sock drawer.

68, 69
Start collecting shopping bags
and you can make a storage
system with a difference.

70
Save apple trays to store
Christmas baubles safely.

Speciality shops

72
Look for catering equipment
suppliers in the Yellow Pages.
You'll be hooked for life!

74, 75, 76, 77
Mass-produced domestic
kitchen units are predictable
and can be pricey. If you are
prepared to shop around,
you'll find exciting alternatives,
designed with a completely
different function in mind. A
vegetable trolley, with removable
baskets is a lifesaver on wheels.
It can hold a lot of anything
and looks good anywhere.
Aero (020 8971 0066) has a
similar model. Under medical
equipment in the Yellow Pages

you will find a brand new
shopping route. Or become a
regular reader of the Classified
section in your local newspaper.
To locate stockists for
butcher's hooks in your area,
consult the butcher's equipment
and supplies section in the
Yellow Pages. Shopping
baskets are available from
Ocean (0870 242 6283).
For other vegetable racks
and freestanding kitchen
units try **The Conran Shop**
(020 7589 7401), **Habitat**
(020 7255 2545), **Heal's**
(020 7636 1666), **The Holding
Company** (020 7610 9160) and
Ikea (020 8208 5607).

79
This early art deco dentist
cabinet is a rare find and came
from a deceased practice. Look
in the Yellow Pages under
furniture—secondhand, or check
the Classified section of your
local newspaper.

80
Ikea (020 8208 5607) and
The Holding Company
(020 7610 9160) stock a large
range of clothing hangers.

82, 83

Mock safety signs are a great way to label off-season clothing in storage. Design your own industrial signs and cover them with plastic. **The London Graphic Centre** (020 7240 0095) stocks easy-to-use sticky plastic.

84

Magnetic strip units for knives and kitchen utensils are available commercially from most kitchen shops.

85

Flexible magnetic strips come in rolls and can be cut into magnets of any length and fixed to walls, wood or tiles with an epoxy adhesive. **Modern Magnetics**, South Africa (0027 11 315 3270) and **H-I-S Enterprise**, South Africa (0027 21 551 5827).

86, 87

Search secondhand furniture shops and the Classified section in your local newspaper to find used office furniture. Coat all the surfaces with metal paint in the colour of your choice to create uniformity and make everything look brand new – even the paint tin! Have school and sport certificates laminated at your local photocopy shop and display them on clipboards. **Kall Kwik** (01895 872000) have photocopy shops nationwide.

Reveal and conceal

88

Old-fashioned concertina files remain the best storage solution for valued documents. And if they're completely transparent, they're right up to date. Call **W H Smith** (01793 695195) or **Paperchase** (020 7467 6200) to find your nearest store.

90, 91

Veil recessed storage space with a sheer blind rather than a solid door for quick visual access. **Habitat** (020 7255 2545), **Ikea** (020 8208 5607) and **Next Home** (0845 600 7000) have a good selection. International style guru Li Edelkoort is the author and publisher of *Interior View*. Order *Interior View 14, Blind Design* from **International Trend Information**, South Africa (0027 31 764 6616).

92

Mesh pockets by **Anne York Interior Designs**, South Africa (0027 11 425 3369).

93

Mesh boxes with lids add order and character to the workplace. Available from **The Holding Company** (020 7610 9160).

94

A reed screen offers an instant storage solution. This one is from **Loft Living**, South Africa (0027 21 442 0088). Others are available from **The Cotswold Company** (0870 550 2233), **Ikea** (020 8208 5607) and **Next Home** (0845 600 7000).

95

To make your own bedside storage bag, sew large melton pockets onto a fleecy strip that fits under the mattress from side to side. Zips provide easy access and privacy.

96, 97

Custom-make organza table strip-covers with a pocket around the edge for cutlery.

Storage on display

98

When it comes to shopping for CD units, don't let your current collection dictate your choice. As your collection grows, you could end up with an unattractive hotchpotch of the small, the cute and the weird. Invest in a good-looking unit with enough space to house your potential collection. A range of designs is available from **Aero** (020 8971 0066), **The Cotswold Company** (0870 550 2233), **Habitat** (020 7255 2545), **Ikea** (020 8208 5607), **Next Home** (0845 600 7000) and **Ocean** (0870 242 6283).

100
First aid box by Roche Smith of **Egg Design** at Milk Products, available from **Space**, South Africa (0027 31 202 4544).

101
Moulded plastic bookshelf from **Innovation**, South Africa (0027 21 418 1154).

102
Clever photo boxes store and display precious moments in the life and times of a fast-growing child. Similar boxes are available from **Paperchase** (020 7467 6200).

103
It's the pinboard principle with a contemporary twist. Turn a translucent shower curtain with pockets into a showcase for your memories. Find them at **The Conran Shop** (020 7589 7401).

104, 105
Look for freestanding display units at **Habitat** (020 7255 2545) and **Ikea** (020 8208 5607). Chisel grooves into a shelf to slip antique cutlery into and onto display.

106, 107
Pot stands are back to simplify our lives! This one is from an antique fair.

108
Stick photographs onto boxes to make them a display item. Find various boxes at **The Cotswold Company** (0870 550 2233), **Habitat** (020 7255 2545), **The Holding Company** (020 7610 9160), **Ikea** (020 8208 5607), **Inventory** (020 7937 2626), **Muji** (020 7323 2208), **Ocean** (0870 242 6283) and **Paperchase** (020 7467 6200).

109
Stacks of your favourite books can revive dull corners and utilize awkward spaces.

useful *addresses*

Furniture and General Storage

Aero

Furniture and accessories, including mobile shelving, metal grids with accessories, stackable wine racks, vegetable trolleys and CD racks

Aero
96 Westbourne Grove
London
W2 5AT
Telephone: 020 7221 1950
Fax: 020 7221 2555

Aero
347–349 King's Road
Chelsea
London
SW3 5ES
Telephone: 020 7351 0511
Fax: 020 7351 0522

Aeromail

Mail order

Furniture and accessories, including mobile shelving, metal grids with accessories, stackable wine racks, vegetable trolleys and CD racks, delivered to your door

Aeromail
Mail order
Telephone: 020 8971 0066
Website: www.aero-furniture.com

The Conran Shop

Furniture, linen, lighting and accessories, including freestanding kitchen units, and translucent shower curtains with pockets

The Conran Shop
Michelin House
81 Fulham Road
London SW3 6RD
Telephone: 020 7589 7401
Fax: 020 7823 7015

The Conran Shop
55 Marylebone High Street
London
W1M 3AE
Telephone: 020 7723 2223
Fax: 020 7535 3205

The Conran Collection

Furniture, linen, lighting and accessories

The Conran Collection
12 Conduit Street
London
W1R 9TG
Telephone: 020 7399 0710
Fax: 020 7399 0711

The Cotswold Company

Stylish storage ideas, including boxes, baskets, coat racks, screens and CD racks

The Cotswold Company
Riverside
Bourton-on-the-Water
Gloucestershire
GL54 2DP

The Cotswold Company

Mail order

Stylish storage ideas, including boxes, baskets, coat racks, screens and CD racks, delivered to your door

The Cotswold Company
Mail order
Telephone: 0870 550 2233
Fax: 01276 609102
Website:
www.thecotswoldco.co.uk

Habitat International

Furniture, linen, lighting and accesories, including canvas organisers, boxes, baskets, mobile wardrobes, hangers, sheer blinds, freestanding kitchen and display units and CD racks

Habitat International
The Heal's Building
196 Tottenham Court Road
London
W1P 9LD
Telephone: 020 7255 2545
Fax: 020 7255 6004
Call or fax the above numbers
to find your local store

Heal's

Furniture, linen, lighting and accessories, including freestanding kitchen units. Heal's also offers an interior design service and a kitchen and bathroom planning and fitting service

Heal's
196 Tottenham Court Road
London
W1P 9LD
Telephone: 020 7636 1666

Heal's
243 King's Road
Chelsea
London
SW3 5UA
Telephone: 020 7349 8411

Heal's
Tunsgate
Guildford
Surrey
GU1 3QU
Telephone: 01483 576715

Heal's
49–51 Eden Street
Kingston Upon Thames
Surrey
KT1 1BW
Telephone: 020 8614 5900

The Holding Company

Specialist storage shops, stocking boxes and crates, baskets, canvas organisers, mobile wardrobes, hangers, shelving on wheels, freestanding kitchen units and vegetable racks

The Holding Company
241–245 King's Road
Chelsea
London
SW3 5EL
Telephone: 020 7352 1600

The Holding Company
Bluewater Mall
Lower Rose Gallery
Bean Road
Bluewater
Dartford
Kent
DA9 9SH
Telephone: 01322 387400

The Holding Company
Fenwick of Newcastle
29 Northumberland Street
Newcastle upon Tyne
NE99 1AR
Telephone: 0191 232 5100

The Holding Company
41 Spring Gardens
Manchester
M2 2BG
Telephone: 0161 834 3400

The Holding Company

Mail order

Specialist storage solutions, including boxes, crates, baskets, canvas organisers, mobile wardrobes, hangers, freestanding kitchen units, shelving on wheels and vegetable racks, delivered to your door

The Holding Company
Mail order
Telephone: 020 7610 9160
Website:
www.theholdingcompany.co.uk

Ikea

Furniture, linens, lighting and accessories, including modular wardrobes, canvas organisers, boxes and crates, baskets, mobile wardrobes, drawstring bags, castors, mobile shelving, hanging shelves, hooks, freestanding kitchen and display units, vegetable racks, sheer blinds and CD racks

Ikea
Telephone: 020 8208 5607
Call the above number for store information and to order

Ikea Birmingham
Park Lane
Wednesbury
West Midlands
WS10 9SF
Telephone: 0121 526 5232

Ikea Brent Park
2 Drury Way
North Circular Road
London
NW10 0TH
Telephone: 020 8208 5600

Ikea Bristol
Eastgate Shopping Centre
Eastville
Bristol
BS5 6NW
Telephone: 0117 927 6001

Ikea Croydon
(The Old Power Station)
Valley Park
Purley Way
Croydon
CR0 4UZ
Telephone: 020 8208 5601

Ikea Edinburgh
Straiton Road
Loanhead
Midlothian
EH20 9PW
Telephone: 0131 118 0500

Ikea Gateshead
Metro Park West
Gateshead
Tyne and Wear
NE11 9XS
Telephone: 0191 461 0202

Ikea Leeds
Holden Ing Way
Birstall
Batley
WF17 9AE
Telephone: 01924 423296

Ikea Nottingham
Ikea Way
Giltbrook
Nottingham
NG16 2RP
Telephone: 0115 938 6888

Ikea Thurrock
(Lakeside Retail Park)
Heron Way
West Thurrock
Essex
RM20 3WJ
Telephone: 01708 860868

Ikea Warrington
Gemini Retail Park
910 Europa Boulevard
Warrington
WA5 5TY
Telephone: 01925 655889

Inventory

Household items for all rooms, including boxes and baskets

Inventory
26–40 Kensington High Street
London
W8 4PF
Telephone: 020 7937 2626
Fax: 020 7938 2626

Inventory
Unit 9 Haymarket Towers
Humberside Gate
Leicester
LE1 1WF
Telephone: 0116 253 2556
Fax: 0116 253 2557

Inventory
10 Harbour Parade
West Quay
Southampton
Hampshire
Telephone: 023 80336141
Fax: 023 80336198

Muji

*Japanese, unbranded goods,
from clothes to household items
and accessories, including
plastic and compartmentalized
boxes*

Muji
Telephone: 020 7323 2208
Call the above number to find
your nearest store

Next Home
Mail order
*Furniture, lighting, linens and
accessories, including baskets,
sheer blinds, screens and CD
racks, delivered to your door*
Next Home
Mail order
Telephone: 0845 600 7000
Website: www.next.co.uk

The Nomad Box Company

*Box manufacturers and factory
outlet, able to make one-off,
bespoke designs*

The Nomad Box Company
Rockingham Road
Market Harborough
Leicestershire
LE16 7QE
Telephone: 01858 464878
Fax: 01858 410175

Ocean
Mail order
*Furniture, accessories and gifts,
including boxes, shopping
baskets, shelving and CD racks,
delivered to your door*

Ocean
Mail order
Telephone: 0870 242 6283

Paperchase

*Boxes, files, paper, card
and stationery*

Paperchase
213 Tottenham Court Road
London
W1P 9AF
Telephone: 020 7467 6200
Call the above number to find
your nearest store

Paperchase
Mail order
*Boxes, files, paper, card
and stationery, delivered to
your door*

Paperchase
Mail order
Telephone: 0161 839 1500

The Pier

*Furniture, textiles and
accessories, including
drawstring bags and
freestanding units*

Telephone: 020 7814 5020
Call the above number to find
your nearest store or request
a catalogue

Pier Direct
Mail order
*Furniture, textiles and
accessories, including
drawstring bags and
freestanding units, delivered to
your door*

Pier Direct
Mail order
Telephone: 020 7814 5004

Shaker Ltd

Traditional Shaker style household items and accessories

Shaker Ltd
72–73 Marylebone High Street
London
W1M 3AR
Telephone: 020 7935 9461

Stationery and Graphic Supplies

W H Smith

Stationer and newsagent with a wide selection of filing devices, including concertina files

W H Smith
Telephone: 01793 695195
Call the above number to find your nearest store

London Graphic Centre

Graphic and art supplies, stationery and office products, including clear plastic

London Graphic Centre
16–18 Shelton Street
Covent Garden
London
WC2H 9JJ
Telephone: 020 7240 0095
Call the above number to find your nearest store

London Graphic Centre

Mail order

Graphics, art supplies, stationery and office products, including clear plastic, delivered to your door

London Graphic Centre
Mail order
Telephone: 020 7240 0095

General Hardware

B & Q

A full range of DIY tools and materials, including castors and wheels, suction and metal hooks and paint

B & Q
Telephone: 0800 444840
Call the above number to find your nearest store

Focus Do It All

A full range of DIY tools and materials, including castors and wheels, suction and metal hooks and paint

Focus Do It All
Telephone: 0800 436436
Call the above number to find your nearest store

Homebase

A full range of tools and materials, including castors, wheels, suction and metal hooks and paint

Homebase
Telephone: 0845 980 1800
Call the above number to find your nearest store

Paint

Crown Paint

A range of paints suitable for different surfaces. A vast colour choice includes shades that can be mixed especially for you

Crown Paint
Akzo Nobel Decorative
Coatings Ltd
Crown House
Hollins Road
Darwin
Lancashire
BB3 0BG
Telephone: 01254 704951
Call the above number to find your local stockist

Dulux Paint

A range of paints suitable for different surfaces. A vast colour choice includes shades that can be mixed especially for you

Dulux Paint
Telephone: 01753 550555
Call the above number for stockist information and product advice

Leyland Paint

A range of paints suitable for different surfaces. A vast colour choice includes shades that can be mixed especially for you

Leyland Paint
Huddersfield Road
Birstall
Batley
West Yorkshire
WF17 9XA
Telephone: 01924 354000
Call the above number to find your local stockist

Photocopy Shops

Kall Kwik

Photocopy shops nationwide aimed at both the business and individual client

Kall Kwik
Telephone: 01895 872000
Website: www.kallkwik.co.uk
Call the above number to find your nearest store, or visit the website

Specialist Shops

Cornucopia Imports

Importers of a wide range of storage accessories, including inflatable hangers

Cornucopia Imports
Eclipse
4B 7th Street
Melville
Johannesburg
South Africa
Telephone: 0027 11 482 5759
Fax: 0027 11 482 5759
E-mail: cornuco@iafrica.com

H-I-S Enterprise

Manufacturers and suppliers of promotional products, including magnetic strips and sheeting

H-I-S Enterprise
Unit 2
Ringer Park
Printers Way
Montague Gardens
Cape Town
South Africa
Telephone: 0027 21 551 5827
Fax: 0027 21 551 3168
E-mail: h.i.s@mweb.co.za

Hollywood Displays

Manufacturers and suppliers of mannequins and shop fitting equipment, including retail clothes hangers

Hollywood Displays
92 Newton Road
Meadowdale
Extension 2
Germiston
Johannesburg
South Africa
Telephone: 0027 11 974 1509
Fax: 0027 11 974 1609
E-mail: info@hollywood.co.za

Inova

Manufacturers and importers of original furniture, including moulded plastic bookshelves

Inova
91 Brick Lane
Shop 11
Dray Walk
London
E1 62L
Telephone: 020 7247 3833
Fax: 020 7247 3878

Mode Information

Supply published reference to the design industry, including Li Edelkoort's book, Interior View 14, Blind Design

Mode Information
Eastgate House
16–19 Eastcastle Street
London
W1N 7PA
Telephone: 020 7436 0133
Fax: 020 7436 0277

Loft Living at Block and Chisel Interiors

Manufacture and supply a range of affordable storage ideas in cardboard, wood, metal and basket materials

Loft Living at Block and
Chisel Interiors
22 Kloof Street
Cape Town
South Africa
Telephone: 0027 21 422 0088
Fax: 0027 21 424 6501
E-mail: loft@iafrica.com

Modern Magnetics

Suppliers of magnetic materials, including magnetic strips and sheeting

Modern Magnetics
16 Richards Drive
Midrand
Johannesburg
South Africa
Telephone: 0027 11 315 3270
Fax: 0027 11 315 4760
E-mail: saie@yebo.co.za

Plastic World

Distributors and fabricators of plastic products, including plastic strip curtains

Plastic World
249 Booysens Road
Selby
Johannesburg
South Africa
Telephone: 0027 11 493 8492
Fax: 0027 11 493 0153
E-mail: info@plasticworld.co.za

WinBlok

Manufacturers of WinBlok, window surrounds made from high-density, low-permeability pre-cast concrete

WinBlok
Telephone: 0027 11 609 8774
Call the above number for a list of suppliers
E-mail: wintec@intekom.co.za

Anne York Interior Designs

Suppliers of a wide range of storage solutions, including mesh pockets

Anne York Interior Designs
28 Clarke Street
Rynfield
Benoni
Johannesburg
South Africa
Telephone: 0027 11 425 3369
or 0027 11 425 3379
Fax: 0027 11 425 3167
E-mail: impact99@global.co.za